Cytherea

Peonies

A LITTLE BOOK OF FLOWERS

Tara Austen Weaver

Illustrations by Emily Poole

 SASQUATCH BOOKS
SEATTLE

For Kaoru-san,
my Japanese host mother,
who shared such beauty with me.
There are not enough flowers in the world
to adequately say
Thank you.

The Peony is known to have been held in such high repute of old as to be accounted of divine origin, an emanation from the moon, endowed with the property of shining in the night, of chasing away evil spirits, and protecting the houses near which it grew.

—HILDERIC FRIEND

Nippon Brilliant

Contents

Origin
of the
Species

Had I but four square feet of ground at my disposal, I would plant a peony in the corner and proceed to worship.

—ALICE HARDING

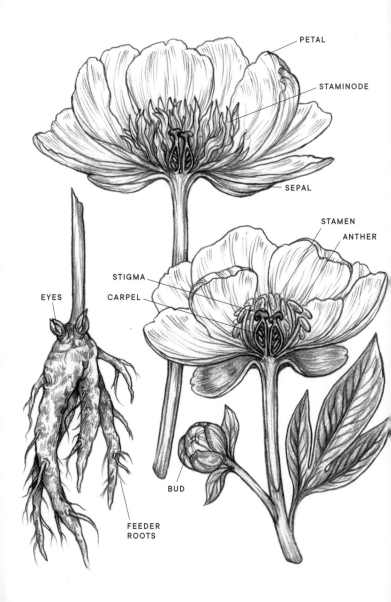

PETAL

STAMINODE

SEPAL

STAMEN

ANTHER

STIGMA

CARPEL

EYES

BUD

FEEDER
ROOTS

Gardeners are a fanciful lot, prone to exaggeration and lyricism, but when it comes to the peony, it's not a stretch to say she is the undisputed queen of the spring garden. Peonies are showstoppers, from the herbaceous (bush) peonies festooned with blossoms so multi-petaled they look like pom-poms, to tree peonies studded with crinkled tissue paper–like blooms that seem improbably fragile, to the grace of a single stem set in a vase, flower petals changing color as they slowly unfurl. It's no wonder that peonies have won hearts around the world.

With all this star power, you might expect peonies to be divas, requiring careful attention and lots of it, but they aren't. Peonies are one of the least demanding flowers you can grow—they require little maintenance yet offer up a stunning display each spring, and do so for decades. I've never met a gardener who regretted planting a peony. The only regret I know is not having room for more.

When we say "peony," we're actually speaking of three different flower types. All peonies are perennials that lose their foliage in winter, but the genus can be divided into three main types: herbaceous peonies that die back entirely, tree peonies that bloom on woody stems, and intersectional peonies that are a cross between the two. While intersectional peonies are relatively new—introduced in the 1960s—herbaceous and tree peonies have a history that goes back thousands of years.

Peonies are considered native to Asia, North America, and Europe, where their territory wraps around the Mediterranean. They thrive in climates that have cool winters—chill hours are required for them to properly develop flower buds. The genus *Paeonia* consists of about thirty species of flowering plants in the family Paeoniaceae. Within that group, however, is a wide variety—from large, showy blooms stuffed with petals that make their way into bridal bouquets and flower arrangements, to the simplicity of a five-petal flower, striking in its minimalism.

While peony forms vary from simple to petal-stuffed and elaborate, the single peony form starts as a sepal-covered bud that swells to reveal a row of petals surrounding a mass of pollen-laden stamens with a carpel in the center. The carpel ends in the stigma, which is where the pollen must be deposited to enable fertilization.

The name peony comes to us from the Greeks. According to Greek mythology, Paeon was a student of Asclepius, the god of medicine. But Asclepius was a jealous teacher. When he saw Paeon using the peony root to heal Hades, god of the underworld, he grew angry. In order to protect Paeon from Asclepius's anger, Hades transformed Paeon into a peony.

There are several versions of this myth. Another variation has Leto, goddess of fertility, telling Paeon about a root on the slopes of Mount Olympus that was helpful to women in labor. It shows that peonies have been valued for their medicinal use as much as for their beauty—and sometimes far more for the former. In both Europe and Asia, peony root has been used to treat a variety of ailments, from epilepsy, to hypertension, menstrual cramping, and spasms. In medieval Europe, the peony was referred to as the "apothecaries' flower," for its wide health applications. In the British Isles, where peonies arrived in the 1200s, children used to wear necklaces made of beads carved from peony root to help with teething and to prevent seizures. Indeed, peony root is still used in Chinese medicine to this day. The flower's earliest use and value was as a health aid. It would be much later that their blooms became as prized as their roots.

The peonies we plant in our garden today carry with them quite a history—from ancient China and Greece, carried in the bags of traders on horseback, in ships across oceans, and in the covered wagons of colonial settlers. Peonies have been through successive waves of popularity and fortune, revered by emperors, sought after by plant collectors, and tended by farmers, backyard gardeners, and painstaking breeders. These days they are beloved by florists and brides.

Peonies have long had associations with love and romance. According to garden writer Julie Martens Forney, "These lovely, luxurious blossoms have come to represent good fortune in marriage." Apparently, roses were the flowers with which to woo a woman—but once he had won her affection, a man would give peonies to his intended bride. This helped secure a place for peonies in bridal bouquets that still continues today; they are thought to confer good fortune, prosperity, and a peaceful, happy marriage.

The peony is also connected to bashfulness and shame. This goes back to a different version of the peony myth from ancient Greece. One day, Aphrodite, goddess of love, found Apollo flirting with a pretty nymph, who hid in the petals of a peony flower to escape the wrath of the angry goddess. For the Victorians, who believed in a language of symbolism behind different flowers, the peony was emblematic of shame. According to *The Meaning of Flowers*, by Claire

Powell, "They are not blushes of modesty which suffuse it with its rosy hues, but the fiery cheeks of guilt, for this flower is the hiding place of a dishonourable nymph."

Paper flower artist Chantal Larocque sums up what has made us love and seek out peonies throughout history—both their gloriousness and their fleeting nature, blooming for just a few weeks each spring. "In my mind, no other flower can compete with the perfection of the peony," she writes in her book *Bold & Beautiful Paper Flowers*. "The silky petals, delicate shape, romantic shades, and graceful foliage make this flower my all-time favorite, and I'm not alone. Brides plan their wedding dates around peony season. Flower enthusiasts plant them all through their gardens. Florists go crazy over all the different shades available . . . Sadly, this bloom can only be enjoyed in nature for a very short time each year."

Peonies may be a brief annual affair, but as any enthusiast will tell you, it is always worth it.

PEONY SCENT

For some, the scent of peonies is one of their best qualities—manufacturers have been trying to capture the elusive sweet fragrance in soaps, perfumes, and lotions for years, with varying results. To stand in front of a pink double peony blossom stuffed with petals in full bloom and breathe the intoxicating fragrance is one of the great delights of spring.

While many peonies have a lovely fragrance, a few have an off-putting odor and some have no scent at all. Those with a scent have a range of fragrances, which fall into the categories of rose, citrus, honey, and musk. The most fragrant flowers tend to be the double white and pink peonies; most single blooms have no smell.

Among the peonies favored for their fragrance are 'Dr. Alexander Fleming' and 'Hermione', pink double blooms stuffed with frilled petals. 'Cora Stubbs' is a Japanese peony, with darker pink guard petals surrounding a fluffy center of lighter pink and white. The award-winning 'Miss America' is a stunning semi-double flower that features white, tissue paper–like petals surrounding a center of golden stamens; the blooms seem to float on a cloud of their own sweet fragrance.

Hermione

Miss America

Cora Stubbs

Dr. Alexander Fleming

Forms of the Flower

This morning the green fists of
    the peonies are getting ready
to break my heart.

—MARY OLIVER

Peony Forms

While the three types of peonies—herbaceous, tree, and intersectional—are based on their botany, peony forms refer instead to the shape of the flowers. While Chinese peony growers recognize a wider variety of shapes, the American Peony Society uses a six-category classification, which is generally used in Europe as well.

Single

The simplest of all forms is the single peony, made up of one or more rows of petals surrounding the center pollen-bearing stamens. The large petals are called guard petals. Wild or species peonies are considered singles and can have up to fifteen petals. There is a simple beauty to this form.

Japanese

The most noted characteristic of the Japanese peony is the staminodes—stamens that have transformed and thickened. The visual impact is like a party in the center of the flower: slightly ruffled, joyous, sometimes multicolored. Because the stamens have become encased in plant tissue, Japanese peonies do not drop pollen.

Anemone

The anemone form is noted for its petaloids, stamens that have lengthened and widened and are approaching petals. Sometimes this makes the blooms look like they have a pom-pom in the center. Other times petaloids are pointy, ruffled, or resemble the small, waving tentacles of a sea anemone. The contrast between the center of an anemone peony and the surrounding guard petals is a striking combination.

Bomb

This peony form does indeed look like a joyous explosion, with so many petals stuffed into each flower head. It is said to be named after an ice-cream dessert (bombe) and looks like a mounded dome served on a saucer. Watching a bomb peony unfurl into bloom is a bit of a clown-car experience—the center petals just keep coming. These are flowers for those who believe you can't have too much of a good thing.

Semi-double

Of all peony forms, the semi-double is the most classic. Stamens are prominent and surrounded by rows of petals, providing contrast in color and texture. Semi-doubles are a grown-up and sophisticated version of the single peony. They look stunning floating in a bowl of water.

Full Double

A double peony has all the excitement and exuberance of a bomb but still may have stamens hidden deep among the petals, which look like the endless ruffled layers of a ballgown. In a double peony, the guard petals take back row to the liveliness of the center, making a pom-pom like none other.

SINGLE

JAPANESE

ANEMONE

BOMB

SEMI-DOUBLE

FULL DOUBLE

Peony Types

All peony cultivars fall into one of three types—herbaceous, tree, or intersectional (also called Itoh) peonies. Each type has a different history, cultural background, and strengths as a plant. This section covers each of the peony types, and recommended cultivars of each (though with thousands of cultivars, there's not nearly enough room to include them all). Consider this an entry point to the wide world of peonies.

HERBACEOUS

Herbaceous, or bush, peonies bloom on soft green stems, which die back in the fall and winter and reemerge in the spring as tiny, red-tinged shoots that grow into a bushy mass about 3 feet tall. They are native to a wide swath of geography that stretches from Japan through China, southern Siberia, southern Europe, and wraps around the Mediterranean, with two species native to North America. When most people hear the word *peony*, it is the herbaceous peonies they think of, a midsize plant with flowers that start out as tight, green balls that swell and unfurl into a variety of forms, from simple species flowers with a single row of petals, to double blooms stuffed with layers like a ballerina's tutu. Years of hybridizing has gifted us with such diversity, it's near impossible to pick a favorite.

The story of herbaceous peonies runs from Asia through Europe to North America. The largest species within the group, *Paeonia lactiflora*, hails from western Asia, where it grows on hillsides and open woodlands in Siberia and the Himalayan region—all areas cold enough in winter for peony flower buds to develop and which receive enough precipitation in summer to keep foliage green. Though appreciated in China, herbaceous peonies have always played second fiddle to the tree peony, which holds a special place in Chinese art and history. It wasn't until herbaceous peonies traveled from Asia to France and eventually to Britain that they found a passionate following. Eventually those first *P. lactiflora* were bred with peonies from southern Europe and the Balkans—cultivars from the *Paeonia peregrina* and *Paeonia officinalis* groups. The results have given rise to a wide variety of flowers that captured the imagination and attention of the world.

France, in particular, contributed greatly to the wealth of peony diversity. In the 1800s, French horticulturalists left their mark through new and exciting peony hybrids, often named after wives, girlfriends, or other family members (dozens of peony names begin with the word *Madame*). The number of peonies that have been passed down with French names, such as Duchesse de Nemours, Modeste Guérin, and Madame Louis Henry, is testament to their contribution.

French horticulturalists were not the only ones contributing to the wide variety of peonies we enjoy today. In the United Kingdom, James Kelway rose to prominence as a breeder of both peonies and gladioli (see page 118). Over his lifetime, Kelway introduced more than a hundred cultivars and provided peony roots to both Queen Victoria and the Impressionist painter Claude Monet, for his famed garden at Giverny.

North America has been the most recent center of herbaceous peony development. Breeders such as Oliver Franklin Brand and his son A. M. Brand started in the late 1880s, developing more than fifty cultivars on their Minnesota farm. Professor A. P. Saunders, who worked to extend the bloom period of the flowers, is responsible for some 265 named cultivars throughout the early to mid–1900s. Others, such as Charles Klehm, at his Charles Klehm & Son Nursery, originally in Illinois, took up the peony breeding torch in the 1950s. The American Peony Society sprang up in the early 1900s, to provide education and organization for the tremendous interest in these new flowers and fanciful forms. These days, in addition to representing peony lovers on a national level and administering an online database of named peony cultivars, regional chapters of the association provide support on a local scale for beginning and experienced gardeners alike.

There is great variety even among the herbaceous peony group. Species peonies—woodland and the North American varieties—are not as frequently grown as their more colorful and decorative cousins, the hybrids. Within the herbaceous group we can see the range of the flower, from the simplicity of wild varieties to the decorative heights and colors that have been achieved through centuries of careful and intentional breeding.

Woodland

The peony season begins with the lesser-known woodland peonies, *Paeonia japonica* and *Paeonia obovata*. These wild flowers are found in the dappled edge of deciduous forests. Blooming in March and April, they benefit from the early season sunlight before most trees have leafed out. Then, in the height of summer, they are shaded from the worst of the heat. Woodland peonies are simple in their bloom form, with colors that range from pink to white. What they lack in showy flowers, however, they make up for in seed pods, which burst open in late summer with a bold display of scarlet and navy. Over time, these flowers naturalize throughout shady areas, providing ground cover and seasonal interest. If your garden lacks the sustained sunlight needed for herbaceous and tree peonies, these lovely woodland cultivars may meet your needs. Suitable for hardiness Zones 3–8.

Paeonia japonica *flower*

Paeonia obovata *seed pods*

North American Peonies

Most peonies hail from China and Europe, but there are two species that are native to North America. *Paeonia brownii*, also known as Brown's or western peony, inhabits the sagebrush desert, pine forests, and stands of aspens in a wide swath from California to Montana. With grayish-green foliage and small-petaled flowers that are a reddish brown and nod downward, Brown's peony blooms in April and May.

Paeonia californica, on the other hand, can be found in the mountains of California and Mexico, growing in the coastal sage scrub and chaparral. *Californica* requires a hot, dry summer period of dormancy, then blooms from January to March. These species are not often grown in gardens, though perhaps that is a shame. They are hearty and low-maintenance, with low water needs. Their flowers are modest when compared to the flashy performers elsewhere in the peony genus, but do beautifully in a rock or desert garden.

Paeonia brownii

Paeonia californica

Herbaceous Hybrids

Most herbaceous peonies belong to the species *lactiflora*, *tenuifolia*, *peregrina*, and *officinalis*. For centuries now, peony breeders have been creating hybrid crosses between these four, resulting in a dazzling array of colors and shapes. There is truly something for every garden, style, and color palette.

Lactiflora

Native to Siberia and the Himalayas, *Paeonia lactiflora* is the most common peony species—the majority of cut peonies sold in the floral industry are from *lactiflora*. Over the years, *lactiflora* has been hybridized to produce a wide variety of shapes and colors, including some of our most popular cultivars. In the garden they are the last group of herbaceous peonies to bloom, but the wait is always worthwhile.

'Krinkled White' (single): An elegant example of the simplicity of the single flower form, this peony seems to float above a 2½-foot bush on long, sturdy stems that generally do not need staking. The 6-inch blooms feature papery white petals surrounding a center of deep-golden stamens much beloved by pollinating bees. A prolific producer, excellent for cut flowers.

'Bowl of Beauty' (Japanese): Aptly named, it features pinkish-mauve guard petals cupping a frilly center of gold staminodes that fade to white as the flower opens. A 3-foot, early blooming bush, with stems strong enough to hold up fragrant 8-inch flowers (no staking necessary), it's a stunner in full bloom.

'Sarah Bernhardt' (double): A delicate froth of pale pink, this is one of the most popular peonies—and for good reason. This 3-foot bush is bedecked with heavy-headed blossoms so full of petals they dip and droop (staking is essential). With a delicate fragrance, this romantic late-bloomer has been winning hearts for more than a hundred years.

'Festiva Maxima' (double): A glorious mound of fragrant, white fluff, this peony is as lovely as it is sweet smelling. An abundance of white petals shot through with the thinnest edging of scarlet, this early bloomer definitely wants staking, as the flower heads are large and abundant. In the garden or in a flower arrangement, these feathery white blooms and their roselike scent attract attention.

Krinkled White

Bowl of Beauty

Sarah Bernhardt

Festiva Maxima

Tenuifolia

Far less common than *lactiflora* is the *tenuifolia*, also called a fernleaf peony—due to finely cut, almost needlelike foliage that creates a feathery look in the garden, where it grows in an airy clump to about 2 feet tall. These peonies are native to Russia, Ukraine, Serbia, Bulgaria, and Romania. The flowers, which can vary in form, tend toward dark red and dark pink, with a bloom period of up to 10 days, starting earlier than most other peonies. Blossoms may be on the smaller side, but a series of these peonies festooned with flowers is a stunning sight. The feathery nature of their leaves, which look almost like carrot greens, makes it appear as though the blooms are floating on a sea of frothy green.

Tenuifolia peonies have been crossed with *lactiflora* cultivars and the result is a number of red-hued flowers that carry on the finely dissected foliage of their parent. Award-winning 'Early Scout' is an example, as are the following cultivars, all of which bloom slightly earlier than the original *tenuifolia* peonies they descend from.

'Merry Mayshine' (single): Featuring all the attributes that make *tenuifolia* peonies unique, this version has finely cut, ferny foliage on 3-foot bushes that provide interest and decoration even when not in bloom. The 5-inch flowers have petals that range from deep red to bright crimson in a cluster around a center of shaggy golden anthers. This early bloomer is a spectacular way to kick off peony season.

'Little Red Gem' (single): This dwarf *tenuifolia* hybrid that grows only 12 to 18 inches tall is an excellent border planting, with feathery green foliage that makes a statement. Like other peonies with *tenuifolia* parentage, their growth pattern creates ferny mounds, bedecked each spring with single-petal red flowers. These shorter bushes (under 2 feet) are sometimes called rock garden peonies.

Merry Mayshine

Little Red Gem

Peregrina

Paeonia peregrina is another less-common peony species—native to southeastern Europe and Turkey—and sometimes called the Balkan peony or the red peony of Constantinople. The foliage, which has nine leaflets, is finely cut, but not quite needlelike. The flowers are a delight—large, cupped blooms of dark red and maroon, nearly 5 inches across; they look almost tulip-like as they surround a center of gold-colored stamens.

This species' main claim to fame is that it has been bred with other cultivars to produce a variety of coral-colored peonies, such as the popular 'Coral Charm', 'Coral Sunset', 'Coral Supreme', 'Pink Hawaiian Coral', and more. Many of these are award winners and deservedly popular. They bloom in varying shades of coral and pink, their petals fading to a light yellow or cream color as they age. The *peregrina* hybrids produce a single flower per stem and have an upright growth pattern that may not need staking.

'Coral Charm' (semi-double): Perhaps the most popular of the coral series, this peony produces tight buds with orangey-pink petals that open into bowl-shaped blooms. A vigorous, reliable grower and early bloomer, it grows to 3 feet and needs no staking. The brilliant-colored blooms are eye-catching in the early spring garden and make excellent cut flowers (they last well under refrigeration; with a vase life of over a week). The coral tone fades to a rich cream as the blooms age, equally beautiful but much more subtle.

'Pink Hawaiian Coral' (semi-double): Blooming in a darker rosy-pink hue than its coral cousins, this version produces ruffled, 5-inch flowers with a lovely scent. The flowers fade from rose pink to apricot to blush. If left on the 3-foot bush, blooms of all colors may be in flower at one time. Plant this fragrant stunner where you can appreciate both the look and the perfume of it.

Coral Charm

Pink Hawaiian Coral

Officinalis

Native to southern Europe—France, Switzerland, the Balkans, Italy, Spain, and Portugal—*Paeonia officinalis* is often called the common peony. With a bloom period that starts mid-May, depending on climate, some *officinalis* hybrids are referred to as Memorial Day peonies, as they can be relied on to bloom in time to celebrate the US holiday, which is in late May.

Paeonia officinalis hybrids include the Flora Plena series—including the award-winning 'Rosa Plena', with large, double, rose-pink blossoms. These hybrids originated in Europe and were brought to the United States by early settlers and carried west in covered wagons. They are often found growing in the yards of old pioneer farmhouses, still blooming after all these years.

'Rosa Plena' (double): Looking like a cheerful mound of ruffles in rose pink, this peony is an early season bloomer with an eye-catching color and spicy fragrance. Its vivid flowers fade to a lighter pink as it ages. 'Mutabilis Plena' is a similar flower in almost translucent pale pink, 'Alba Plena' blooms in white, and 'Rubra Plena' in strong red.

'Buckeye Belle' (semi-double): The curved dark-red petals—almost burgundy in color—cups a tangle of golden stamens, an eye-catching contrast in tone and texture. The unique colors continue into autumn, when its leaves turn a striking maroon. Like most *officinalis* hybrids, this semi-double is a sturdy grower (2½ feet tall; no staking necessary) and a reliable early bloomer.

Rosa Plena

Buckeye Belle

TREE PEONIES

Tree peonies are native to China and its environs, where they are affectionately referred to as the King of Flowers. They have woody stems and are deciduous, losing their leaves every winter. Blooming early in spring, they are a standout in the garden—growing up to 6 feet with flowers up to 8 inches across, dazzling in both their size and delicacy. They are also called *mudan*, their common name in Chinese, or woody peonies, due to the nature of their stems.

According to an ancient Chinese legend, the peony spirit Gejin fell in love with a young scholar who was fond of growing flowers. She transformed herself into a beautiful woman in order to marry him. The couple was happy and in love—and over time had two children together. One day, however, the scholar could not find his wife. An important guest was expected and Gejin feared the guest would see that she was an apparition. She fled with the couple's two children, leaving two large peony bushes in their place. The scholar went into mourning for his love, but they were never reunited.

Despite this sad story, peonies have been celebrated in China throughout history. They are thought to symbolize wealth, honor, peace, and beauty—and they have strong ties to royalty. Peonies were a favored flower of Chinese emperors, often used as a decorative motif in porcelain, tapestry, and painting, and can even be found decorating ancient Chinese tombs. It was the Tang dynasty (618–907), a period of prosperity where art and culture flourished, that peonies rose to prominence and were even put under the legal protection of the emperor. The peony gardens in Luoyang (page 124) were planted at this time, when China's only empress,

GROWTH FORM OF TREE PEONY

Wu Zetian—known for both her cleverness and her cruelty—banished the peony from her capitol at Xi'an because it failed to obey orders and bloom on her birthday.

Peonies are often paired with the phoenix in Chinese art, especially in embroidery. Peonies are considered the king of flowers and the phoenix the king of birds; together they symbolize wealth and happiness. Some believe that items decorated with peonies would promote their chances of prosperity, status, and happiness. The peonies we plant in our gardens today come from a revered and ancient lineage.

Tree peonies can grow from 4 to 6 feet, becoming statuesque additions to any landscape. Their range of colors is striking, and many have petals that blend or darken toward the center. As tree peonies grow and mature, their blooms get larger. Their woody stems provide the structure to support large flowers, which makes them a showstopper when they bloom in April and May.

Within the tree peony group there are numerous species, but three of the most common are *suffruticosa*, *rockii*, and *lutea*. While tree peonies originated in China, and remain extremely popular there, many of the cultivars widely available for sale in the United States are Japanese introductions.

Suffruticosa

Hailing from the central plains of China, *Paeonia suffruticosa* is the largest of the three species. They are known for their range of colors—from white to pink, maroon, and magenta—and for their appealing fragrance as well. Within this group there are numerous flower forms, from blooms with a single row of petals, to bomb forms exploding with delicate layers, and great diversity in shape and color. Most tree peonies fall into *suffruticosa*, a group that has grown larger due to years of hybridization. Members of *P. suffruticosa* are suitable to hardiness Zones 4–9.

'Multicolored Butterfly' (semi-double): Looking a bit like a candy confection, these butterflies in full bloom feature 6-inch blossoms of pale-pink ruffled petals with darker mauve striping surrounding lemon yellow anthers and a pale-green carpel. Growing up to 6 feet and blooming with a beguiling fragrance, 'Hua Hu Die'—as it is known in China— makes an excellent focal point in the spring garden.

'Shima-nishiki' (semi-double): A rare peony with striped petals, its unusual and striking look is due to a bud mutation on an all-red peony. The result is a new, variegated (irregularly colored) cultivar whose flowers may be red, white, and most often striped. Blossoms can grow to be 7 inches wide and bloom on a medium-size bush (3½ to 5 feet tall and wide). This midseason bloomer puts on an unforgettable show—in the colors of a peppermint stick.

'Shintenchi' (semi-double to double): A vision in pink, this 4-foot, award-winning bush carries 10-inch blooms that seem to float like clouds. Centers of golden anthers are surrounded by layers upon layers of petals, like taffeta, that fade from dark pink to pale on the outer edges.

'Shintenchi', which means "new heavens and earth" in Japanese, was the first peony bred outside North America to win the American Peony Society's Gold Medal (1994).

Multicolored Butterfly

Shima-nishiki

Shintenchi

Rockii

Also referred to as Gansu tree peonies, for the province in northwestern China where they originated, the Chinese name for these flowers translates to "purple flare," as the petals turn purple at the base. Their leaves tend to be more narrow than other cultivars and they are cold hardy, suitable to Zones 2 and 3. They can also be grown in semi-shade and will still flower. If you are looking to fill a dappled garden area, they are a magnificent option.

'Guardian of the Monastery' (semi-double): This stunning example of *rockii* purple flare is a standout in any garden, festooned with flowers of up to 7 inches, with dark red-purple that fades to mauve and then white toward the edges of the petals. A shaggy center of golden anthers sets off the flowers that bloom on 4-foot plants with a mild but beguiling fragrance.

'Baron Thyssen-Bornemisza' (semi-double): A ballerina tutu of a flower, this pale-mauve confection darkens to purple at the base, a trait of its parentage. Ruffled petals surround a mound of golden stamens on flowers that can grow up to 10 inches. Named for a wealthy Dutch-born businessman, these 4-foot plants are sturdy and make for excellent cut flowers.

'Dojean' (semi-double): This hybrid has flares that skew deep red rather than purple, with white petals and a pink-crimson center surrounded by golden anthers. It was developed by Sir Peter Smithers—the British diplomat, spy, and plant breeder said to have inspired Ian Fleming's James Bond. Flowers grow 8 inches across and bloom on 7-foot-tall, vigorous shrubs.

Guardian of the Monastery

Baron Thyssen-Bornemisza

Dojean

Lutea

Hailing from the Himalayas, these peonies flower in shades of gold and yellow. With narrow leaves and flowers that sometimes dangle downward like golden bells, they are less cold hardy (they do well in Zones 7 and 8) but can grow up to 6 feet. They have been hybridized, which has led to a beautiful palette of cream, yellows, golds, reds, and purple. These peonies also bloom a few weeks after other tree cultivars and are better suited to damp conditions than most other peonies.

'High Noon' (semi-double): Sparkling in pale yellow, this hybrid shows off its golden tones. Each 3-inch flower darkens to a small red flare at the base with a short ruff of golden anthers. Fast growing and tall—up to 5 feet—this hardy, late-season bloomer has a sweet, citrusy fragrance and cheerful appearance.

'Iphigenia' (single to semi-double): Named after a princess from Greek legend, this dark-red peony grows up to 5 feet, festooned with ruffled blooms that are striking in their dramatic coloring. This midseason bloomer makes a statement in flower arrangements or in a garden, with deeply colored petals surrounding a loose center with pale-yellow anthers.

'Theresa Anne' (double): A relatively new introduction (2013), this hybrid is graceful, with pale-pink to apricot petals with darker rose flares as they circle a center of golden anthers. A somewhat short bush (3–4 feet tall) that grows wide with pale-green foliage, it flowers heavily, each bloom looking like a beacon of spring happiness before it fades to a cream color.

High Noon

Iphigenia

Theresa Anne

INTERSECTIONAL (ITOH)

Itoh or intersectional peonies are a cross between the herbaceous peony and the tree peony. Botanists spent years trying to cross the two. Herbaceous and tree peonies do not bloom at the same time, however, so making a successful cross was quite difficult. Finally, in the late 1940s, Japanese botanist Dr. Toichi Itoh produced seven hybrids. Unfortunately, he did not live to see his flowers bloom, but his work was continued by others. American horticulturalist Louis Smirnow bought some of those original crosses from the widow of Dr. Itoh and brought them to the United States, where the work to develop new flower cultivars continued.

The peony has always held a favored position in Japanese culture—considered to symbolize happiness, marriage, bravery, and prosperity. As in China, the flowers play a role in art and culture. Peonies have long been a favorite subject of visual artists—seen in the famous woodblock prints of the 1800s, and in a modern-day form of art, the tattoo.

Itoh or intersectional peonies share many herbaceous traits—their foliage and stems die back in winter, their growth habit and size is bushy, not exceeding 3 feet. The flowers, however, resemble those of tree peonies in their wide variety of colors and their delicacy. Intersectional peonies also produce secondary buds, which means their bloom period is long. A mature intersectional peony may have as many as fifty blossoms in a season.

When they were first introduced to the market, intersectional peonies were so rare and sought after that prices were high—up to $1,000 for a single plant. A reliable supply has brought prices down, but intersectional peonies are still popular and sought after. Not only are their colors and flower shapes stunning, but they also bloom later than most herbaceous cultivars, extending the peony season as long as possible.

'Strawberry Blush' (single): A vision in pink, these flowers feature rose-colored petals irregularly streaked with maroon and white around a spray of yellow stamens and carpels tipped in red. A recent introduction (2010), this sturdy, midseason bloomer feels crisp and modern, like a fresh, spring breeze.

'Cora Louise' (semi-double): Looking like layers of white lacey petticoats, the ruffled petals surround a center with purple flares—a sign of *Paeonia rockii* genetics—and wispy golden anthers. The lightly fragrant flowers grow up to 10 inches and are abundant. With attractive foliage on a 2-foot bush, this midseason bloomer is deservedly popular.

'Bartzella' (double to semi-double): A classic in lemon yellow, this cultivar brightens up any garden. Pale-gold petals deepen in color toward the base, with reddish flares around a center of deep-golden anthers. Flowers can grow up to 9 inches and vary from double to semi-double on a single bush. A midseason bloomer on a 3-foot sturdy bush, no staking is necessary. This multiple award-winner caused a sensation when it was first introduced in 1986 and remains a solid fan favorite today.

'Hillary' (semi-double): This glorious peony is like two flowers in one—huge blooms of dusty red fade to a creamy pink with red centers. On the bush they present a two-tone effect that is a visual knockout. Lightly fragranced, it is an award-winner and sure to be the center of attention in any garden.

'Sonoma Amethyst' (semi-double): This midseason bloomer presents numerous lavender blooms on a 3-foot bush. A vigorous grower that blooms abundantly in many-petaled flowers of pinkish purple that darken toward the base of the petals. Generous golden anthers surround a reddish-pink carpel, which makes for an unusual, eye-catching bloom.

Strawberry Blush

Cora Louise

Bartzella

Hillary

Sonoma Amethyst

Peonies make fine sentinels lining walkways or a lovely low hedge. After its stunning bloom, the peony's bushy clump of handsome glossy green leaves lasts all summer, and then turns purplish-red or gold in the fall, as stately and dignified as any flowering shrub.

—CATHERINE BOECKMANN

Peony Growing & Flower Culture

Peonies probably are going to be the longest-lived perennial in your garden; they will outlast you. These are things that get passed on for generations—some of them have made it over the oceans when people immigrated . . . and are still going today.

—DARREN HEIMBECKER

Preparing to Plant

Peonies are resilient flowers—healthy plants can grow for more than a hundred years. Because of this, and because peonies do not enjoy being moved, make sure to plant them in a suitable location and take the time to prepare the site well.

Peonies grow in hardiness Zones 3–8, with some cultivars able to survive Zone 2 as well. Peonies want at least a bit of cold in the winter, as they need the chill to help form flower buds. The soil pH level should be neutral (pH 6.6–7.3). Clay or boggy soil is best avoided, as it can cause the tubers to rot in winter. Likewise, avoid areas in your garden that are watered by an automatic sprinkler system, as daily watering is unnecessary for peonies.

Peonies need well-draining soil and full sun (6–8 hours a day) but are best sheltered from strong winds that can damage their slender stems. Tree peonies may appreciate shade from the midday heat, especially in the warmer climates. Some gardeners even shade their tree peonies with waxed sun parasols, as is often done in China and Japan. This helps extend blossom life from a few days to a week or more and preserves their color from fading.

The best time to plant bare-root peonies is fall, when the weather has cooled and the plants are dormant (September and October, depending on your location). You'll want to have all peonies planted at least 6 weeks before your first frost date. This will give the peony a chance to settle in before winter. If you are relocating a mature plant (not recommended but sometimes unavoidable), stick to the same mid-autumn timeline.

If you must plant in spring, look for the potted peonies available at that time of year. While you can find suppliers selling bare root tubers in springtime, they do not grow as well as fall-planted specimens and can be more susceptible to diseases.

Peonies want to take center stage, so don't crowd them. They do not like to compete for soil moisture or nutrients, so don't plant grasses or shrubs too close—spacing and airflow is important to avoid fungal diseases. Herbaceous and Intersectional peonies will grow up to 3 feet tall and about as wide; make sure to allow 4 feet of space between plants. Tree peonies can grow up to 7 feet tall and about 5 feet wide, so plan accordingly.

Because peonies will likely be in place for decades to come, it's worth investing some time and care in their planting site. Take stock of your soil type and consider what amendments are needed. Clay soil will need compost and rock dust or gypsum, to help with drainage. Sandy soil will benefit from compost and organic matter, to help with nutrition and water retention. The goal is a loose mixture that gardeners call friable loam.

If you are unsure about the quality of your soil, consider getting it tested (a local agriculture extension office or nursery should be able to recommend a good lab). Acidic soil will need supplemental lime added to bring up the pH to neutral level (pH 6.6–7.3). If your soil is not ideal for peonies, you could consider building raised beds or mounds and bringing in soil that would be better suited for the plants.

Most herbaceous peonies need some sort of support, as their flowers are heavy, their stems are thin, and any rain at all can bring them down. Double or bomb peonies are particularly prone to toppling. Single, semi-double, and anemone varieties may not need additional support.

There are a variety of metal supports designed for peonies—most resemble the wire "cages" used to support tomatoes. Actual tomato cages can be used, but most will need to be cut down as they are a bit too tall for peonies (use wire clippers and cut the verticals just above the smallest support ring at the bottom; this will give you a shorter cage and a wider base so you won't cause as much damage in the root zone). Wire peony supports need to be installed early in the season before the plants have reached 6 inches tall.

Some people prefer to support peonies using a "grow-through grid." This is a round wire grid on stakes that is placed over the flower, which then grows through the wires. Grids are helpful as they support each stem and flower individually—as opposed to cages, where the stems generally lean to one side or another. The trade-off is that cages tend to be a bit sturdier than grids. Most growers prefer one method or the other. If using grids, place them on the ground just as peony shoots are emerging in the spring and let them grow through the wires, raising them up on their stakes only when the shoots are tall enough.

If you don't want to invest in cages or grids, it is possible to plant sturdy stakes or bamboo poles, each about 4 feet long, in a circle surrounding the peony, about 6 inches out from the plant and 6 inches apart. Starting at a height of about 6 inches, run twine around the stakes and go slightly

GROW-THROUGH GRID

PEONY CAGE

STAKES AND TWINE

upward with each circle. If you bury the stakes 1 foot underground, you should have a useful height for peony support (about 3 feet).

Planting Peonies

Many tubers are purchased directly from growers and shipped to the purchaser's home, so if your tubers arrive at an inconvenient time—or when the ground is frozen, and you are not able to plant them promptly—store them in the refrigerator in the packaging materials they arrived in and plant them as soon as you can.

If your tubers arrive dry or wrinkled, soak them in water for a few hours before planting. If there is slight whitish or greenish mold on the tubers, it can be washed off. Any rotten or softened tubers, however, should be returned to the nursery or the grower that sold them.

Peonies need cold, so don't worry about them freezing after planting. Do keep an eye on them the first winter, however, because the freezing soil can shift them out of position. (If that happens, cover with a bit of extra soil until the ground thaws and you can reposition.) Unlike other flowers, peonies should not be heavily mulched or excessively protected from the cold. A too thick layer of soil may keep them from flowering in the spring.

Woodland, Herbaceous, and Intersectional Peonies

To plant peony tubers, dig a hole about 2 feet across and 2 feet wide, loosening the soil all around to a depth of about 1½ feet. Add any needed amendments, mixing thoroughly with the native soil in the hole. Add about ½ cup of bone meal, to encourage root development and flower growth. If your soil is acidic, now is the time to add lime to raise the pH level.

One of the issues with peonies is that tubers planted too deeply will not bloom. Position your tuber so it is less than 2 inches below the surface of the soil—and even less if you live in a warmer climate (Zones 7 and 8 can plant as little as ½ inch under the soil, while Zones 4 and 5 should aim for

HERBACEOUS
PEONY TUBER

1½ inches). Nestle the tuber into the soil with the eyes facing upward, cover as needed, and tamp the soil down around the root to eliminate any air pockets. Water in well. Make sure to check after watering, to see if the soil has settled and to make sure the peony is not positioned too deep. Do not mulch in winter, as peonies need the cold for proper bud development.

If planting potted peonies, position the peony so that the top of the soil in the pot is level with the native soil of the planting site and water in well. Check later to see if the soil has settled and reposition, if needed.

Tree Peonies

To plant tree peony roots, dig a hole about 1 foot across and 2 feet deep, loosening the soil all around. Add any needed amendments, mixing thoroughly with the native soil in the hole. Add about ½ cup of bone meal, to encourage root and flower growth.

As many tree peonies are grafted, position the root so that the graft is 4 to 6 inches below the soil surface. When planting tree peonies that are not grafted, make sure the stem-root junction is at least 2 inches beneath the surface of the soil. Tamp down the soil around the plant and water in well. After the soil settles, check to make sure the positioning of the peony has not shifted.

Peony Care

Peonies generally thrive on benign neglect; they are one of the lower-maintenance perennials in the garden. Once established they will produce for years to come with little assistance. Winter and spring rains should provide adequate irrigation, but once the warmer, drier weather comes on, water your peonies every other week for the first year or two. Peonies want to dry out between watering. Unless you are experiencing an extended drought, live in an exceedingly dry area, or your peony seems distressed, no additional water should be needed.

Likewise, peony fertilizer needs are quite low. Take stock of your soil—sandy soil will want a little more assistance than richer soil. Fertilizer can be applied either in the fall, at cleanup time (this is preferred), in spring after shoots have emerged, or early summer after blooming has finished. You don't need to fertilize more than once a year, and perhaps not even that often.

Fertilizer should be spread thinly in a circle around the drip line (do not apply to the stem area). Use either a balanced, slow-release fertilizer like 5–5–5 or 10–10–10, a low-nitrogen flower blend, or a combination of compost with a bit of bone meal mixed into the soil around the planting. Avoid any use of weed killer or pesticides, even nearby to peonies, as it can damage them. Keep the planting area free of weeds or competing plants to allow the peonies to thrive.

In the fall, the foliage of herbaceous peonies will turn beautiful shades of gold and orange. Enjoy the autumnal color for as long as it lasts. As the seasons change and the leaves begin to droop, however, cut the foliage back to the base of the stem and dispose of it (not in a home composting system). Leaves that are left to decompose can harbor diseases and pests. Woodland peonies should also be cut back (you can allow their navy-blue seeds to drop to the ground to naturalize or collect them to plant elsewhere). The stem area of woodland and herbaceous peonies should be left bare: no mulching.

Intersectional peonies should be cut back as well, but not as far as herbaceous peonies—just to the woody portion of the stem. If it's unclear where this is, allow the plant to die back on its own and remove the withered leaves.

Tree peonies should not be cut back in autumn. As leaves begin to fall, they should be removed and disposed of (not in a home composting system). Make sure not to damage any buds on the tree peony while removing the leaves. If leaves don't come off easily by hand, use pruning shearers. Do not cut back any of the woody growth.

Don't mulch tree peonies unless you are growing them in a very cold climate. In Zone 2 or 3, however, you can mulch peony roots with straw or pine needles (avoid bark or wood chips), making sure to remove the mulch once the cold weather has passed. If you live in snow country, be wary of heavy snow buildup that may break or damage tree peony branches in winter.

Pruning Tree Peonies

Tree peonies do not require much in the way of pruning. In late winter or early spring, before bud break, check the plant for dead wood. Any dark wood can be cut back to the closest live bud (use an angle cut, slanting down and away from the bud; this helps the water drain off). Look at the base of the plant for any weak or spindly growth and remove this as well. If shaping is desired, this is the time to do it, but in general only minimal pruning is required of tree peonies. Some tree species tend to be vigorous growers. As time goes by, removing some of the upright stems may help promoting a more bush-like shape. As always, make sure to cut with clean pruning shears, and remove and dispose of any cuttings (not in a home compost system), as they may harbor disease if left in place.

Ants on Peonies

While a common garden myth says that ants found on peonies help the flowers blossom, this is not accurate. Ants are attracted to the sugars, also called honeydew, that is secreted by herbaceous peony blossoms. They do not help the flowers, per se, but the presence of ants likely scares away other insects that might do greater damage. Ants are an integral participant in peony season; just make sure to remove any stowaways on cut peonies before you bring them indoors.

Failure to Bloom

An occasional issue with peonies is failure to bloom, which may occur for a number of reasons. It can take several years for peonies to settle in and begin to flower—if the plant is in its first 2 to 3 years in that location, patience may be required. Too much shade may be an issue as well. If the peony is not getting enough sunlight, consider moving it to a brighter location (wait until fall for any transplanting). Excessive fertilizer can also be a problem, as adding too much nitrogen will result in leaf growth but not flowers. Peonies often thrive with no fertilizer at all, or only occasional applications (fertilizer is best applied in the fall; use either a balanced fertilizer, or one with more phosphorous than nitrogen). Also, peonies planted too deep may not bloom. Tuber eyes should be no more than 2 inches below the surface of the soil. Late frosts or botrytis blight (see page 130) can also harm peony buds and prevent them from blooming.

Deadheading Peonies

During bloom season, remove spent blossoms once they have faded, unless you are interested in seed production. Intersectional and herbaceous peonies should be cut back to the first large leaf, so the stem is not protruding. Tree peonies should be cut just below the blossom. This allows the plant to put energy into root growth and not focus on seed production (the seed heads, however, are attractive and some people prefer to let them develop).

Pests and Diseases

Peonies are, on the whole, quite disease resistant. Most problems can be warded off with good growing practices: plant flowers so there is adequate air flow between them (3–4 feet apart); do not use overhead watering sprinklers; water early in the day, so there is time for the moisture to evaporate; make sure to plant in well-draining soil; and remove old leaves and withered foliage at the end of the season. This should prevent most disease issues. If you do run into problems, however, the pests and diseases glossary on page 130 should help you identify probable causes.

Making the Most of Peonies

I equate peonies with love
because they're the first
blooms of summer.

—ISAAC MIZRAHI

Harvest

Peony plants are slow to mature—it will be 2 to 3 years before it's wise to cut flowers from newly planted herbaceous and intersectional peonies. They require a bit of patience, but it will reward you with generous blooms for decades to come. As always, use clean scissors or pruning shears to avoid the risk of spreading disease when cutting any flowers.

Like most flowers, peonies should be cut early in the morning when the temperature is still cool. Buds should be closed, but soft—the squishable texture of a marshmallow is ideal for peony buds. If buds are picked while too firm, they may not open in the vase; too soft or partially open and they won't have much of a vase life before they begin to lose their petals.

Make sure to leave at least three sets of leaves on the plant stalk when cutting herbaceous and intersectional blooms; this will help the tubers stay strong and healthy. For the longevity of the plant, do not cut more than half the blooms off a peony each season.

Because herbaceous peonies attract ants, shake off the stems or plunge the bud heads into a bucket or basin of cold water once or twice to make sure these insects are not brought into the house along with the flowers. Place the stems in water as soon as possible.

Tree peonies (which do not attract ants) can also be cut for flower arranging, but make sure to only cut the green stem and avoid removing any of the woody growth. Cut just below the bloom and use in centerpieces and other low arrangements, or float in a bowl; the flowers will look stunning.

Before arranging your flowers, hold the bottom of the stems under water—in a bucket or the sink—and trim off about ½ inch, cutting on a 45-degree angle. The angle cut allows for maximum water absorption, and the water "seals" the cut and makes sure it's not exposed to air as you transfer them to your vase or other receptacle. Changing the water daily, or at least every few days, will prolong their vase life, as will keeping them out of direct sunlight or unnecessary heat. Peonies generally have excellent vase life, lasting a week or more.

Because peonies are cut before they are in full bloom, you will need to plan ahead if you are harvesting for a special occasion. Buds cut at the "marshmallow" stage generally open within 2 to 3 days. If you need to speed up this process, place stems in warm water in a warm room. To slow the opening, cool water and a cool, dark room should do the trick.

If you need to hold the flowers longer, refrigeration at 34 degrees F is ideal (kitchen refrigerators, which generally run between 37 degrees and 40 degrees F, can also be used). Make sure not to refrigerate peonies with any sort of fruit, as the ethylene gas emitted by ripening fruit will cause the flowers to open faster. Because peony season is so short, if you have an abundance of blooms, consider cutting and refrigerating the extras. Unopened flowers, cut at the marshmallow bud stage, should last a few weeks if well wrapped in newspaper or a plastic bag with some paper towels inside

(this helps absorb moisture). Lay flat on the refrigerator shelf, check regularly for any rot or withering, and when ready to use, recut the stems under water and the blooms should open.

Displaying Peonies

Peonies are a delight to use in arrangements—they have strong stems, stunning blooms, and a reasonably long vase life. Whether it is a simple bunch of matching blooms, a single flower in a small bud vase, or an elaborate decorative arrangement, peonies attract attention.

The great variety that peonies offer in the garden also provide a wide range of options in the vase. You can select by form, by color, or mix and match. A simple bundle of 'Coral Charm' or 'Sarah Bernhardt' blooms is pure delight, whereas more complicated blooms like 'Bowl of Beauty' or 'Guardian of the Monastery' bring their own celebration of color and texture and need little added. While there certainly are a few discordant matches, it's impressive how often peonies complement each other—even across forms and color families. The best part about growing a selection is having enough blooms to get creative and play with.

What makes peonies so stunning is also sometimes their weakness: heavy blooms can cause stems to bend and break. For this reason, consider how you want to support the flowers. Either use a vase with a narrow neck, which will allow stems to lean and be supported, or enlist some florist tricks to help along the way.

For larger peony arrangements, flower grids are essential. These are usually made of wire and fit into the neck or opening of a vase or other arranging vessel. These can be purchased from floral supply shops or online sellers—or you can make your own with a small bit of chicken wire, bent to fill the space (use wire cutters to cut to size). It's also possible to make lovely, organic-looking grids from lengths of wood or bamboo fastened in a cross pattern (use twine or flexible ties to secure the joints). If you are working with heavy stems, you may want to use a grid as well as a floral frog—a small metal disk covered in spikes that rests at the bottom of a vase or bowl and helps secure stems for greater stability. Whatever you use, make sure to affix it to the vase or vessel with florist tape or sticky clay so it doesn't slip around.

Alternately, you can make a single-use grid by using tape— florist tape is ideal, but painter's tape or even clear tape will work in a pinch. Form a crisscross pattern across the neck of the receptacle that you will be using—just make sure to fill with water and dry the rim prior to applying tape, or it will not stick properly. Once the grid is finished, insert the stems of your flowers and let the crisscross pattern help to hold them upright.

To avoid possible bacterial contamination, vases and any supports used for flower arranging (frogs or chicken wire) should be washed with detergent and a weak bleach solution before being used. Fill clean vases with cool water, adding commercial flower food if you choose (or a pinch of sugar can stand in for flower food). Make sure to remove any leaves that would sit below the waterline in the vase, as they will begin to rot and shorten the life of your flowers.

When designing a larger floral arrangement—to display on a mantlepiece or side table—it's important to consider that heavier, multi-petaled peony heads will be weighty and need to be placed lower in the arrangement. Use lighter branches or decorative grasses to create size and volume in the back (privet, dogwood, ferns, eucalyptus, ninebark, or Mexican feather grasses are all good options). Smaller, compatible flowers and leaves can fill out the middle. Peonies mix well with hellebores, anemone, lupine, sweet peas, and roses of a coordinating color—both full size and small spray roses—among many other options. An arrangement of lavender lilacs and pink 'Sarah Bernhardt' peonies is a stunning, late-spring combination that will perfume a room (though lilacs do not have much of a vase life). Also, do not rule out mixing peonies of different sizes, colors, and forms—simple, single form flowers can play off an elaborate bomb or double bloom with beautiful results.

Peony blooms are so stunning, they are a perfect excuse to think outside the box. While traditional arrangements are delightful, nontraditional approaches often show the flowers off to their best advantage. Imagine a long table or windowsill with a row of identical small glass jars or bud vases, each with a single peony bloom—either all the same cultivar or gradations of color. Wide champagne coup glasses can be used in a similar manner for an unexpected but elegant installation. And tree peonies, in particular, look stunning when floated in a wide, shallow bowl (blue and white Chinese porcelain makes a striking choice, as does celadon pottery, both green and blue). Peony season is so short, it's worth celebrating while you can.

Preserving Peonies

The flower's fleeting nature makes any peony lover want to make the most of their blooms. Happily, there are a few ways to preserve them to get full use of your flowers until peony season comes around again.

Edible Petals

The lovely colors of peony petals lend themselves to a great many decorative uses. Make sure to use only garden-grown flowers, or peonies from a trusted source that grows organically—commercial plants may have been treated with sprays or chemicals you would not want to consume. Petals will last 1 or 2 days after being removed from the flower heads, but it's best to store them in the refrigerator until you are ready to use them.

Here are some favorite ways to incorporate edible petals into your meals and parties:

· Top salads with peony petals for a bit of whimsy and color. Make sure to sprinkle them on the salad after it has been dressed for best effect, as salad dressing will weigh down the petals and make them stick to the bowl.

· Peonies can make a beautiful decoration for frosted cakes or cupcakes—either loose petals scattered at random or used as whole flowers for a more elaborate and artistic display (make sure to remove the flower centers and any stem before serving, as these should not be eaten). Apply petals and flowers no more than a few hours before serving.

- Freeze petals into ice cubes to be used for party drinks—
  either in the drinks themselves, or to fancy up a bucket for
  wine or champagne (just be prepared to refresh with new
  ice to keep it looking festive as the event goes on).

Peony Simple Syrup

Makes 2 cups

This pale-pink syrup makes a refreshing spritzer when mixed with sparking water, or as an ingredient in a cocktail (a natural match to gin or vodka). Garnish with lemon or lime, a slice of cucumber, or sprig of tarragon or basil. Use the most fragrant petals you can; it's like spring in a glass.

1 cup packed peony petals, any withered or brown bits removed (ideally use a portion of dark-pink petals for color)

2 cups granulated sugar
Juice of half a lime or lemon

Gently rinse the peony petals to remove any dirt, debris, or pests and place them in a large heat-proof bowl. Add 2 cups boiling water, to cover all the petals, and let steep 6 hours or overnight. Strain the peony mixture through a mesh strainer lined with cheesecloth, muslin, or even a few paper towels.

Pour the liquid into a saucepan and add the sugar, stirring over a medium heat until the sugar is dissolved. Remove from heat and add the citrus juice. Once the syrup has cooled, pour into a clean bottle or jar and store in the refrigerator. Use within 2 months.

Peony Petal Jam

Makes 3 to 4 pints

This jam features a delicate peach-strawberry-like flavor. Make sure to use at least a portion of darker-pink petals for a beautiful color.

4 cups fresh peony petals, any withered or brown bits removed
5 cups boiling water
3 cups granulated sugar

Juice of 1 lemon (about 3 tablespoons)
One 3-ounce package of liquid pectin

Gently rinse the peony petals to remove any dirt, debris, or pests and place them in a large heat-proof bowl. Add the boiling water, to cover all the petals, and let steep 6 hours or overnight (you may want to place a small plate on top to keep the petals submerged). Strain the peony mixture through a mesh strainer lined with cheesecloth, muslin, or even a few paper towels. The liquid will smell green and herbaceous at this point.

Pour 3½ cups of the peony liquid into a saucepan set over medium heat and add the sugar, stirring to mix. As the sugar dissolves, add the lemon juice, which will bring out the peony color. Add the pectin and stir to mix. Bring to a boil and boil for 5 minutes before pouring into sterilized pint or half-pint canning jars with sterilized two-part canning lids, leaving a ½-inch headspace. At this point you can ether process according to safe canning guidelines, or store in the refrigerator and use within 3 months.

Peony Petal Body Scrub

Makes 2½ cups

Another way to extend the life of your flowers is to transform them into a body scrub. Many peonies have a lovely scent, but if yours don't you can add your own fragrance—either through using a fragrant base oil like almond or coconut, or by adding a few drops of essential oil with a scent you like. This scrub makes an excellent gift for friends and family.

½ cup tightly packed peony petals, removed from their flower heads

2 cups granulated sugar

⅔ cup base oil (either sweet almond oil, coconut oil, or a neutral oil such as grapeseed)

5 tablespoons liquid glycerin

6 to 8 drops of essential oil in a scent of your choosing (optional)

Place the fresh petals in the bowl of a food processor and add the sugar. Pulse the sugar and petal mixture in short bursts until the petals have broken down (do not let the processor run continuously). The petals should be in tiny pieces and well dispersed throughout the mixture.

Spread the sugar mixture evenly on a large baking sheet or other platter to dry (you may want to line it with a sheet of parchment paper for easier cleanup). Remove any large pieces of petal that might remain. Allow the mixture to air dry for 1 or 2 days.

$\longrightarrow$

Pour the sugar mixture into a large, dry bowl and mix in the oil, glycerin, and the essential oil (if using). Pack into clean glass jars and keep in a cool, dry place. To use, spread on damp skin in the bath or shower and rub to exfoliate before rinsing clean (you may want to use a mesh drain insert in your bath or shower if you are concerned about bits of petal going down the drain). The scrub will last for up to 4 months.

How to Dry Peony Flowers

If you'd like to preserve peonies for decorative uses, it is possible to dry the flower heads. This is best done with double or bomb-style peonies. Cut your flowers early in the day, before they have been warmed by the sun. Select blooms that are newly opened (you can also dry buds that are starting to open and show color). Cut 6-inch stems and remove any extra leaves. Tie each stem with twine or a rubber band

and hang upside down, making sure the blooms are not touching (a coat hanger or dowel can be useful for drying several stems at once with adequate space between). Hang the flowers in a cool, dark space for several weeks, until the flowers are dry.

It's also possible to dry flower heads using silica gel, which is a granular desiccant available at craft supply shops. You'll need to pour a few inches of silica into the bottom of a container, place the flower on the gel, then slowly and carefully sprinkle more gel over the flower, allowing it to sift between each petal until the flower is covered (a large slotted spoon or a strainer or colander can be useful to sift the gel). It will only take a few days to dry, but be careful when removing the flower from the gel.

If you want to dry a flower with a long stem, you'll need a tall, narrow container and a large quantity of silica (which can be reused to dry additional flowers). Flowers that are dried without stems can be wired into place for dried flower arrangements.

The colors of the peonies will fade a bit as they dry. Flowers dried with silica gel will retain more color intensity than those that are air dried. Make sure to keep dried blooms out of direct sunlight when you use them in crafts or arrangements, to prevent fading.

Flower
Viewing

The fattest and most scrumptious of all flowers, a rare fusion of fluff and majesty, the peony is now coming into bloom.

—HENRY MITCHELL

Cricket Hill Garden

THOMASTON, CONNECTICUT

Nestled in the hills of Litchfield County lies Cricket Hill, a family-run nursery that has been selling and specializing in tree peonies since 1989. Run by the Furman family, with two generations now involved in the business, Cricket Hill offers such poetically named cultivars as 'Golden Summit of a Snowy Mountain', 'Guardian of the Monastery', 'Black Dragon Brocade', and 'Icy Heart of a Vast Ocean'. A visit to their nursery in bloom season will plunge you into a world where charming paper umbrellas are set up throughout the 6-acre display garden to shade and protect the flowers. The Furmans are deeply knowledgeable about the peony growing world, having trialed more than five hundred peonies to find the cultivars they sell. Bloom period begins in mid-May, with the Japanese and hybrid tree peonies, and goes until about June 20. The Furmans call their nursery Peony Heaven; it is an apt description.

TreePeony.com

Peony's Envy

BERNARDSVILLE, NEW JERSEY

If there is one place a peony lover could be on a warm evening as May turns into June, it would be the annual Peak Bloom Party at Peony's Envy in Bernardsville, New Jersey. Held at the 7-acre nursery and display garden, this buffet dinner and flower celebration allows attendees to dine surrounded by seven hundred different peony cultivars. Those who cannot attend the dinner can still visit and stroll the grassy paths that lead through a woodland setting that is magical in full bloom. The nursery offers Friday night picnics, hands-on workshops on peony propagation, and private events. Accessible from both New York City and Philadelphia, Peony's Envy is the creation of horticulturalist and peony educator Kathleen Gagan. In addition to the display garden, 12 acres of production fields may be available to pick your own flowers. Bloom period at Peony's Envy begins in late April, with species peonies, moving on to tree cultivars, herbaceous, and intersectional peonies, ending about the second week of June.

PeonysEnvy.com

Nichols Arboretum

ANN ARBOR, MICHIGAN

Each spring, peony aficionados in the Midwest flock to Ann Arbor for bloom season at University of Michigan's Nichols Arboretum. Established in 1922 with a gift from peony collector Dr. W. E. Upjohn, a graduate of the university, the arboretum features more than five hundred different peony cultivars. The collection is the largest public collection of historic herbaceous peony cultivars in North America and presents a unique opportunity to view so many different flowers in one place, over half of which are no longer commercially available. The tree and intersectional peonies begin blooming in late April, but peak bloom for the herbaceous garden is generally between Memorial Day and the summer solstice. The garden also plays host to a series of events, including an annual concert of Chinese flower songs during peony season and an outdoor performance of Shakespeare in the arboretum.

Peony.mbgna.umich.edu

Adelman Peony Gardens

BROOKS, OREGON

Not far from Salem, Oregon, in the lush Willamette Valley, lies Adelman Peony Gardens, otherwise known as Peony Paradise. The gardens began in 1993, when Carol and Jim Adelman started planting peonies on their mixed crop farmland. Their vision was to provide peony lovers with an experience not available elsewhere—the opportunity to see the wide variety of peony flowers planted in large color blocks. The Adelmans now grow nearly five hundred cultivars on 25 acres, including a 2-acre demonstration garden with herbaceous, tree, and intersectional cultivars. Their flowers regularly win Best in Show at the annual American Peony Society convention. Visitors are welcomed during their May 1 through June 15 bloom season and can wander the flower fields, purchase cut or potted peonies, and order bare root tubers. The Adelman's cultivar selection is wide and it's rare to be able to see so many different flowers in situ. The stunning fragrance and beauty of a field of blooming peonies is not to be missed; it is paradise, indeed.

PeonyParadise.com

Peony Showgarden
LEMELERVELD, NETHERLANDS

With more than two thousand types of peonies, the Dutch Peony Showgarden is the largest collection of herbaceous and intersectional peonies in the world. A very recent addition to the peony world, it was founded in 2010 and moved to a new site in 2017. Laid out in tidy beds with grass pathways, the garden feels more like a botanic display garden, which is exactly its purpose—to show potential buyers (wholesalers and retail) the wide possibilities that exist within the family of peonies. A 2-hour drive from Amsterdam, and equally accessible from western German cities such as Düsseldorf and Bonn, the garden's mid-April spring bloom period is an embarrassment of floral riches. The Dutch have for years been huge suppliers of peonies for the cut flower industry; two-thirds of the peonies grown in Europe come from the Netherlands. The garden is open to the public by appointment only.

PeonyShowgarden.com

Kelways Plants

LANGPORT, SOMERSET, UK

If you were a summer passenger on the London to Penzance rail line in the early 1900s, your train might pause at a special, seasonal station called Peony Valley Halt. There you could disembark and stroll the blooming peony fields grown by James Kelway as part of his nursery, founded in the 1850s. James was an avid plantsman, starting in the trade as a teenager, and expanded his nursery until it comprised 200 acres of cultivated plants and flowers. Kelway was known for his work breeding peonies, and the valley started out as selection ground for his seedlings. Today Peony Valley is a collection of favorite and historic cultivars, many of which have won awards at flower shows such as Chelsea for more than a hundred years. The nursery still operates, with Dave Root overseeing the current peony program. Kelways is the largest grower of peonies in the UK, and the name lives on in the many stunning varieties they've developed over the years, such as 'Kelways Glorious', 'James Kelways', and 'Kelways Scented Rose'.

Kelways.co.uk

Whistling Gardens

WILSONVILLE, ONTARIO, CANADA

If you've ever wanted to get married surrounded by one of the largest collections of peonies, Whistling Gardens, a private botanical garden located southwest of Toronto in Canada, should be at the top of your list. Owned by Darren and Wanda Heimbecker, who specialize in conifers, woody plants, and peonies, the garden began in 2007 as nothing more than a cornfield. It now hosts a collection of 1,300 different peony cultivars, thanks to donations by award-winning peony grower and former president of the Canadian Peony Society David J. Maltby, and the Cook family of Blossom Hill Nursery. This original donation has since been expanded and now comprises the largest peony collection in North America, including herbaceous, intersectional, and tree peonies. The full gardens cover 20 acres and they do indeed host weddings, as well as other special events. Peony bloom season is May 15 through June 30.

WhistlingGardens.ca

Peony Garden Tokyo

TSUKUBA, JAPAN

The Chinese have a special claim to peonies, but the Japanese have their own history with the flower as well, having cultivated them since the eighth century. To experience Japanese peony artistry, plan a visit to Peony Garden Tokyo in the town of Tsukuba on the northern edge of the city, during their bloom period of mid-April until early June. Founded in 1989, the garden has grown its collection to fifty thousand cultivars, the largest collection of tree peonies in Japan. Peak bloom features twenty thousand peonies blooming at once. A green oasis in Ibaraki Prefecture, the garden is designed around a crater lake that provides habitat for kingfishers and herons. While many peony gardens consist of fields of blooming flowers, Peony Garden Tokyo is a beautifully designed landscape that includes kalmia trees, azaleas, rhododendron, irises, and Alpine roses, all blooming in season. A stunning scarlet-colored bridge spans the waterway and an on-site restaurant nestled in the 15–acre garden offers local cuisine and tea made from peony flowers.

PeonyGardenTokyo.com

Winter-Blooming Peonies

JAPAN

Visitors to Japan in January and February have the unique opportunity to see winter-blooming peonies. Originally developed in Japan more than 300 years ago, Kan-botan are peonies that flower in winter, but they are challenging to grow and the bloom time is dependent on the weather each year. As a result, the Japanese have developed a way of cultivating Fuyu-botan (winter peonies). These are spring-blooming peonies that are chilled in a temperature-controlled environment, then brought out to bloom in January. This mimics spring and causes the flowers to blossom; they are considered good luck for the New Year. To protect the flowers from snow, each plant is nestled beneath a hut-like shelter made from woven straw. To see these blooming peonies with their gold-colored shelters decorated with a dusting of snow is a rare and beautiful experience.

Winter-blooming peonies can be seen at a number of places in Japan.
- Toshogu Shrine in Ueno Park, Tokyo
- Tsurugaoka Hachimangu Shrine, Kamakura
- Sekkoji Temple, Nara
- Yotaku-ji Temple, Hyogo Prefecture

Luoyang National Peony Garden

LUOYANG, CHINA

The ultimate destination for peony lovers must certainly be the Luoyang National Peony Garden in China, where the peonies are considered the "finest under heaven." Located in the west of Henan Province, in the central part of the country, Luoyang is one of the four ancient capitals of China. There the Luoyang gardens feature more than one million peony plants, with examples of 1,200 different cultivars. The collection is heavily weighted toward Chinese introductions, but international cultivars are included as well. The gardens cover 113 acres with highlights such as the Peony King, a 116-year-old tree peony that is 8 feet tall and produces blooms up to 8 inches across. Luoyang's history with peonies dates back to the Sui Dynasty (581–618), when peony cultivation in the area began. It is also home to China's National Peony Genetic Storehouse, the country's research and breeding program. Bloom period in Luoyang is in April, with a Peony Festival from April 1 to May 5.

Merry Mayshine

Glossary

ANEMONE: a peony flower form with outer guard petals surrounding inner petaloids.

ANTHER: the end portion of a flower stamen that produces pollen.

BOMB: a peony flower form with outer guard petals surrounding an inner mounded explosion of petals; said to be named after the ice-cream dessert called bombe.

BUD BLAST: when a flower bud turns brown or fails to open; may be caused by a variety of circumstances, including botrytis blight, late frost, or lack of water.

BUD BREAK: point of time at which a flower or plant bud begins to open.

CARPEL: female reproductive portion of the plant (not present on all peonies). Once fertilized, the carpel transforms into a seed pod.

CROSS: two different plants may be crossed to produce a new hybrid; the process of hybridizing plants by cross-pollinating and growing out the seed that is produced.

CROWN: the point at which the roots of a plant produce stems; the root crown. Roots and stems have different vascular systems, and it is important that the crown not be buried too deep, as it will be deprived of oxygen and may fall victim to crown rot and other diseases.

CULTIVAR: a cultivated species of a plant, intentionally created through breeding.

DEADHEADING: removing withered flowers from a plant after it has bloomed.

DOUBLE: a peony form that features many petals; stamens may be present but rarely visible.

DRIP LINE: outer circumference of a bush or plant; the line at which water or dew drips off.

EYES: plant buds located on a root or tuber.

GRAFT/GRAFTED: the process by which two plants are fused together in order to take advantage of the desirable traits belonging to each. Most frequently strong roots (rootstock) will be used to support the upper portion (scion) of a particularly desirable flower or tree that may have known root weaknesses.

GUARD PETALS: a row of outer petals on a peony that surround the center of the flower.

HYBRID: a plant cultivar created by crossing two parent plants to pass on specific desirable traits.

INTERSECTIONAL: also called Itoh peony (see *Itoh*).

ITOH: a hybrid peony developed by crossing herbaceous and tree peonies; named after Japanese horticulturalist Toichi Itoh, who first pioneered this flower cross. Also called intersectional peony.

SINGLE: a peony flower form that features a single row of guard petals around an open center.

SEMI-DOUBLE: a many-petaled peony form; not as elaborate as the double peony.

SPECIES: original form of peony, featuring a single row of petals.

STAMEN: the male reproductive portion of a plant, located in the center of the flower; made up of the anther (upper, pollen-bearing portion) and the filament (stem on which the anther rests).

STAMINODES: modified stamens due to hybridization; stamens encased in plant tissue.

VARIETY: naturally occurring plant or flower that grows true to form; not an intentionally cultivated or hybridized version.

Pests & Diseases

BOTRYTIS BLIGHT: Browned or blackened areas on peonies is likely the work of *Botrytis paeoniae*, which overwinters in plants from the previous summer. Older infections may develop a gray fuzz on top of the infected areas. This is one of the most common ailments with peonies. If infection is found, remove the entire plant promptly and burn or dispose of it in the garbage (not in a home composting system). You should always source disease-free peony roots from healthy stock and consider cultivars that are disease resistant.

HOPLIA BEETLE: A tiny, oval-shaped beetle with a dark-brown head and brown-green iridescent wings. Eggs are laid in the soil and overwinter; adults emerge in early spring. They are drawn to white, yellow, apricot, and pink colors, chewing holes that damage buds and flowers. Hoplia beetles have a single life cycle, so the danger exists only from March to May. Chemical sprays are not recommended; the best solution is to handpick the beetles and dispose of them in a bucket of soapy water. Alternately, just clip off any flower heads that have been infected.

LEAF BLOTCH (also called red spot or measles): Small red or purplish spots on young peony leaves shortly before bloom time, caused by a fungal pathogen and mostly affecting older varieties. The small blotches grow and the underside of the infected leaves turn brown and look withered. Blotch does not necessarily kill a peony, but it can weaken the plant if it becomes an annual event. If blotch becomes an issue, you may want to replant with modern, resistant varieties.

NEMATODES: Gardens are full of these microscopic worms. Many nematodes do not cause damage, but a few can become a problem for peonies—stunting the plants, causing yellowing and small wartlike galls on stems or roots. Foliar nematodes can cause leaf discoloration that starts yellow before turning red or brown. The damage is likely to appear on older leaves, spreading to new growth and neighboring plants, and is generally passed via water (be careful when watering). Peonies suffering from nematode infections should be removed and disposed of in the garbage (not composted). Do not replant in that area for at least 1 year—turn over the soil and keep clear of weeds to reduce risk of reinfection.

PHYTOPHTHORA BLIGHT: Flourishing in cool and wet conditions, this fungus attacks the roots of peonies, resulting in blackened and rotted stems, buds, and flowers. If disease does occur, remove all affected areas of the plant and any surrounding soil. If the roots are infected, the entire plant must be removed and disposed of (not in a home composting system). Make sure to clean your tools after doing so.

POWDERY MILDEW: A white or grayish bloom on leaves and stems that infects a variety of plants, usually late in the summer. Powdery mildew is a common fungus: it is unsightly, but it does not generally harm the plant. If the leaves seem otherwise healthy, it's fine to leave them until regular end of summer removal. If the leaves are withering, cut back to the base and dispose of it in the garbage (not in a home composting system). As with many fungal infections, prevention is key. If powdery mildew is a reoccurring problem, consider if your peony is planted in the best spot.

THRIPS: An insect that can cause damage to peony petals, leaves, and stems (order: Thysanoptera). They suck the liquid out of plant tissue, resulting in scarring, discoloration, and dead areas. Any infected branches or buds should be removed immediately and disposed of in the garbage (not compost). There are no preventative measures, apart from good plant health and hygiene, but some gardeners report success with insecticidal soap or neem oil when infections do occur.

STEM ROT: Caused by the fungus *Sclerotinia sclerotiorum*, stem rot thrives in wet, cool conditions. Peony shoots that suddenly wilt and fall over, or crowns that are covered by a fluffy white mold, or those that develop black spots on the stem area may have been affected by stem rot. Prevention is key. In case of infection, diseased plants should be removed and destroyed (not composted). Remove the soil around the plant as well, to prevent reinfection, and replace with a less susceptible plant.

TOBACCO RATTLE VIRUS (TRV): An infection that can appear as a series of concentric circles of yellow and green on peony leaves, or shaded, wavy yellow lines or chevrons, or sometimes even purple or red. Symptoms may appear in the cooler months and disappear in summer. Even if only one part of the peony is showing symptoms, the entire plant will be infected and should be removed and disposed of (not in the compost). Remove the soil around the infected plant as well. It's possible for commercial growers to not know their plants are infected, so keep an eye on any new plantings in case they may be transporting the virus.

VERTICILLIUM WILT: A soil-based fungal disease that causes wilting and yellowing leaves, which can turn brown as the plant dies. If these leaves drop to the ground they can spread the fungus. Dark streaks may be visible in the stem. Peonies infected with verticillium wilt may appear to recover, only to have symptoms the following year. If infection occurs, plants should be removed as soon as possible and disposed of (not composted). That area should not be replanted with peonies; choose a crop that is not prone to verticillium wilt infections.

In the Victorian era, people were fascinated with the intimate relationship between ants and a peony flower's unfurling. This intimate partnership of ants with the blooms brought peony meaning to embody female purity and chastity.

—JULIE MARTENS FORNEY

Salmon Dream

Resources

As any peony lover knows, these flowers can quickly become a passion, a collection—or both. It's not uncommon to get hooked and find yourself trolling grower websites trying to track down tubers for favorite peony blooms (a comprehensive database of named cultivars can be found on the American Peony Society website, while local society chapters can provide support and education).

Societies & General Resources

AMERICAN PEONY SOCIETY
The American Peony Society, established in 1903, hosts an online cultivar registry and offers a wealth of information on cultivating peonies on their website. They host an annual convention, as well as publishing a number of books and periodicals, including the Directory of New Cultivars. AmericanPeonySociety.org

THE PEONY SOCIETY

Based in Europe, The Peony Society offers growing information, cultivar registration, community support, and discussion boards on their website. The site is in English but has translation capabilities.

PeonySociety.eu

American Peony Society's List of Top 20 Peony Cultivars

(selected by members in 2020)

Top pick: 'Bartzella'

2 'Pastelegance'
3 'Etched Salmon'
4 'Coral Charm'
5 'Old Faithful'
6 'Red Charm'
7 'Lemon Chiffon'
8 'Sarah Bernhardt'
9 'Garden Treasure'
10 'Buckeye Belle'
11 'Mackinac Grand'
12 'Coral Sunset'
13 'Salmon Dream'
14 'Cora Louise'
15 'Mrs. Franklin D. Roosevelt'
16 'Athena'
17 'Bowl of Beauty'
18 'Festiva Maxima'
19 'First Arrival'
20 'Duchesse de Nemours'
21 'Henry Bockstoce'

Peony Suppliers

A & D Nursery
6808 180th St. SE #8340
Snohomish, WA 98296
360-668-9690
ADPeonies.com

Adelman Peony Gardens
5690 Brooklake Rd. NE
PO Box 9193
Salem, OR 97305
503-393-6185
PeonyParadise.com

Blossom Hill Nursery
681 Fife's Bay Rd.
Selwyn, ON K9J 6X4
Canada
705-742-9923
BlossomHillNursery.com

Caledon Hills Peony Farm
16849 Kennedy Rd.
Caledon, ON L7C 2H9
Canada
519-927-3734
CaledonHillsPeonyFarm.com

Cricket Hill Garden
670 Walnut Hill Rd.
Thomaston, CT 06787
860-283-1042
TreePeony.com

Dutch Girl Peonies
5254 Queen Victoria Rd.
Beasley, BC V0G 2G2
Canada
250-359-7142
PeonyFarm.ca/wp

Gilbert H. Wild and Son
2944 State Hwy. 37
Reeds, MO 64859
888-449-4537
GilbertHWild.com

Hollingsworth Peonies
PO Box 233
Maryville, MO 64468
HollingsworthPeonies.com

Peony's Envy
34 Autumn Hill Rd.
Bernardsville, NJ 07924
PeonysEnvy.com

Swenson Gardens
PO Box 209
Howard Lake, MN 55349
763-350-2051
SwensonGardens.com

Whistling Gardens
698 Concession 3 Townsend
Wilsonville, ON N0E 1Z0
Canada
519-443-5773
WhistlingGardens.ca

Further Reading

Peonies, by Pamela McGeorge, photographer Russell McGeorge (Firefly Books, 2006).

Peonies: Beautiful Varieties for Home and Garden, by Jane Eastoe, photographer Georgianna Lane (Gibbs Smith, 2018).

Peony: The Best Varieties for Your Garden, by David C. Michener and Carol A. Adelman (Timber Press, 2017).

The Gardener's Guide to Growing Peonies, by Martin Page (Timber Press, 1997).

Alba plena

Shimane Sedai

TARA AUSTEN WEAVER is an award-winning writer, editor, and avid gardener. She is author of several books, including *Orchard House* (finalist for the 2016 Washington State Book Awards), *Growing Berries and Fruit Trees in the Pacific Northwest*, and the Little Book of Flowers series. She is trained as a Permaculture Designer, Master Gardener, and Master Composter/Soil Builder. Tara writes frequently about gardening, agriculture, food, art, travel, and social justice. More information can be found on TaraWeaver.com.

EMILY POOLE was born and raised in the mountain town of Jackson Hole, Wyoming. After receiving her BFA in illustration from the Rhode Island School of Design, she returned west to put down roots in the mossy hills of Oregon. She can be found exploring tidepools and cliffsides, gathering inspiration, and making artwork about our fellow species and how to be better neighbors with them.

Printed in China

SASQUATCH BOOKS with colophon is a registered trademark
of Penguin Random House LLC

26 25 24 23 22   9 8 7 6 5 4 3 2 1

Illustrations: Emily Poole | Editor: Hannah Elnan
Production editor: Jill Saginario | Designer: Anna Goldstein

Library of Congress Cataloging-in-Publication Data
Names: Weaver, Tara Austen, author.
Title: Peonies : a little book of flowers / Tara Austen Weaver.
Description: Seattle, WA : Sasquatch Books, 2022.
Identifiers: LCCN 2021002911 | ISBN 9781632173621 (hardcover)
Subjects: LCSH: Peonies.
Classification: LCC SB413.P4 W43 2022 | DDC 635.9/3344—dc23
LC record available at https://lccn.loc.gov/2021002911

Grateful acknowledgment is made to the following:
Page 91: Courtesy of Isaac Mizrahi. Reprinted by permission
by the author.

ISBN: 978-1-63217-362-1

Sasquatch Books
1904 Third Avenue, Suite 710
Seattle, WA 98101

SasquatchBooks.com

MIX
Paper from
responsible sources
FSC® C001701
www.fsc.org